The Poetry of John Bunyan

Volume II (of III)

John Bunyan was born in 1628. His fame emanates from the allegorical book The Pilgrim's Progress. A classic of the English language.

A committed non-conformist Bunyan's life covered two seminal periods in English history: The English Civil War and the Restoration of Charles II. He fought in the former and was subject to over 12 years in prison during the latter.

Whilst this caused great hardship, even more so one expects to his young wife and their children, his spirit and determination to remain dutifully worshipping of his faith was undoubted and resolute.

It is with particular pleasure that we bring you perhaps a side to his life that has not been fully appreciated. His poetry. Across their verses and number are works of quite remarkable thought.

John Bunyan died in 1688, just short of his 60th birthday and is buried in Bunhill Fields in London.

Index of Contents

CAUTION TO STIR UP TO WATCH AGAINST SIN

The first eight lines one did commend to me,
The rest I thought good to commend to thee:
Reader, in reading be thou rul'd by me,
With rhimes nor lines, but truths, affected be.[1]

8 April 1684

I.

Sin will at first, just like a beggar, crave
One penny or one half-penny to have;
And if you grant its first suit, 'twill aspire,
From pence to pounds, and so will still mount higher
To the whole soul: but if it makes its moan,
Then say, here is not for you, get you gone.
For if you give it entrance at the door,
It will come in, and may go out no more.

II.

Sin, rather than 'twill out of action be,
Will pray to stay, though but a while with thee;
One night, one hour, one moment, will it cry,
Embrace me in thy bosom, else I die:
Time to repent [saith it] I will allow,
And help, if to repent thou know'st not how.
But if you give it entrance at the door,
It will come in, and may go out no more.

III.

If begging doth not do, sin promise will
Rewards to those that shall its lusts fulfill:
Penny in hand, yea pounds 'twill offer thee,
If at its beck and motion thou wilt be.
'Twill seem heaven to out-bid, and all to gain
Thy love, and win thee it to entertain.
But give it not admittance at thy door,
Lest it comes in, and so goes out no more.

IV.

If begging and promising will not do,
'Twill by its wiles attempt to flatter you.
I'm harmless, mean no ill, be not so shy
Will ev'ry soul-destroying motion cry.
'Twill hide its sting, 'twill change its native hue,
Vile 'twill not, but a beauty seem to you.
But if you give it entrance at the door,
Its sting will in, and may come out no more.

V.

Rather than fail, sin will itself divide,
Bid thee do this, and lay the rest aside.
Take little ones ('twill say) throw great ones by,
(As if for little sins men should not die.)
Yea SIN with SIN a quarrel will maintain,
On purpose that thou by it might'st be slain.
Beware the cheat then, keep it out of door,
It would come in, and would go out no more.

VI.

Sin, if you will believe it, will accuse,
What is not hurtful and itself excuse:
'Twill make a vice of virtue, and 'twill say
Good is destructive, doth men's souls betray;
'Twill make a law, where God has made man free,
And break those laws by which men bounded be.
Look to thyself then, keep it out of door,
Thee 'twould entangle, and enlarge thy score.

VII.

SIN is that beastly thing that will defile
Soul, body, name, and fame in little while;
'Twill make him, who some time God's image was,
Look like the devil, love, and plead his cause;
Like to the plague, poison, or leprosy
Defile 'twill, and infect contagiously.
Wherefore beware, against it shut the door;
If not, it will defile thee more and more.

VIII.

SIN, once possessed of the heart, will play
The tyrant, force its vassal to obey:
'Twill make thee thine own happiness oppose
And offer open violence to those
That love thee best; yea make thee to defy
The law and counsel of the deity.
Beware then, keep this tyrant out of door,
Lest thou be his, and so thy own no more.

IX.

SIN harden can the heart against its God,
Make it abuse his grace, despise his rod,
'Twill make one run upon the very pikes,
Judgments foreseen bring such to no dislikes
Of sinful hazards; no, they venture shall
For one base lust, their soul, and heav'n and all.
Take heed then, hold it, crush it at the door,
It comes to rob thee, and to make thee poor.

X.

SIN is a prison, hath its bolts and chains,
Brings into bondage who it entertains;
Hangs shackles on them, bends them to its will,
Holds them, as Samson grinded at the mill,
'Twill blind them, make them deaf; yea, 'twill them gag,
And ride them as the devil rides his hag.
Wherefore look to it, keep it out of door,
If once its slave, thou may'st be free no more.

XI.

Though SIN at first its rage dissemble may,
'Twill soon upon thee as a lion prey;
'Twill roar, 'twill rend, 'twill tear, 'twill kill out-right,
Its living death will gnaw thee day and night:
Thy pleasures now to paws and teeth it turns,
In thee its tickling lusts, like brimstone burns.
Wherefore beware, and keep it out of door,
Lest it should on thee as a lion roar.

XII.

SIN will accuse, will stare thee in the face,
Will for its witnesses quote time and place
Where thou committedst it; and so appeal
To conscience, who thy facts will not conceal;
But on thee as a judge such sentence pass,
As will to thy sweet bits prove bitter sauce.
Wherefore beware, against it shut thy door,
Repent what's past, believe and sin no more.

XIII.

SIN is the worm of hell, the lasting fire,
Hell would soon lose its heat, could SIN expire;
Better sinless, in hell, than to be where
Heav'n is, and to be found a sinner there.
One sinless, with infernals might do well,
But SIN would make a very heav'n a hell.
Look to thyself then, to keep it out of door,
Lest it gets in, and never leaves thee more.

XIV.

No match hast sin save God in all the world,
Men, angels it has from their stations hurl'd:
Holds them in chains, as captives, in despite
Of all that here below is called Might.
Release, help, freedom from it none can give,
But he by whom we also breathe and live.
Watch therefore, keep this giant out of door
Lest if once in, thou get him out no more.

XV.

Fools make a mock at SIN, will not believe,
It carries such a dagger in its sleeve;
How can it be (say they) that such a thing,
So full of sweet, should ever wear a sting:
They know not that it is the very SPELL
Of SIN, to make men laugh themselves to hell.
Look to thyself then, deal with SIN no more,
Lest he that saves, against thee shuts the door.

XVI.

Now let the God that is above,
That hath for sinners so much love;
These lines so help thee to improve,
That towards him thy heart may move.
Keep thee from enemies external,
Help thee to fight with those internal:
Deliver thee from them infernal,
And bring thee safe to life eternal.
AMEN.

FOOTNOTE:

1. This same sentiment is well expressed in Bunyan's verses at the conclusion of the Pilgrim, part First.

'Nor let my figure or similitude
Put thee into a laughter or a feud;
Leave this to boys and fools, but as for thee,
Do thou the substance of my matter see.'

A DISCOURSE OF THE BUILDING, NATURE, EXCELLENCY, AND GOVERNMENT OF THE HOUSE OF GOD; WITH COUNSELS AND DIRECTIONS TO THE INHABITANTS THEREOF.

'Lord, I have loved the habitation of thy house, and the place where thine honour dwelleth.'–Psalm 26:8

ADVERTISEMENT BY THE EDITOR

Beautiful in its simplicity is this treatise on the Church of Christ, by John Bunyan. He opens, with profound knowledge and eminent skill, all those portions of sacred writ which illustrate the nature, excellency, and government of the house of God, with the personal and relative duties of its inhabitants. It was originally published in a pocket volume of sixty-three pages, by G. Larkin, 1688.

What is the church? is a question upon which all the subtilty of jesuitic schoolmen and casuists has been exhausted, to mystify and mislead the honest inquirer in every age. The Jews, Papists, Greeks, English, have each claimed the divine favour as being exclusively limited to their respective sects. Apostolic descent has been considered to depend upon human ceremonies, instead of its consisting in a similarity of mind and conduct to that of the apostles, through the powerful influences of the Holy Spirit upon the heart. Judging from this latter mode, we conclude that Bunyan the brazier was very nearly related to, and descended from, Paul the tentmaker, and the other apostles. But we form a very different judgment as to the descent of Bonner and other persecuting bishops.

A visible church of Christ is a congregation of the faithful, who having personally and individually given themselves to the Saviour, unite together to promote each other's spiritual happiness. Such were the churches to whom the epistles in the New Testament were addressed. The instructions given to this spiritual community, in the following treatise, are drawn solely from the sacred volume, and are full of peace and righteousness–tending purely to its happiness and prosperity. If these directions were strictly and constantly followed, our churches, notwithstanding the liability of the members to err, would each present 'a little heaven below.'

The officers in these communities are–I. Bishops, or preaching elders, to dispense the word and ordinances; a plurality in every church, to supply the services of such as suffered under affliction of body, or were imprisoned for conscience-sake. II. Ruling elders, to assist the preachers–to admit the serious inquirer, or shut out the profane backslider, and to re-admit the penitent–to watch over the members, that they be diligent in their worldly callings, that there be no drones or idlers–to heal offences–to feed the church with admonitions, and to visit and comfort the sick. III. Deacons, to manage the temporal affairs–provide for the Lord's table and for that of the bishops and elders–and to distribute the alms to the infirm and needy. IV. Female deacons, to nurse the sick, and direct their attention to that home where there shall be no more sorrow; and generally to aid the deacons and elders.

The duty of the private members is to walk humbly with God, and to be devoted to each other's happiness. In all these particulars Dr. John Cotton of New England, in his 'True Constitution of a Visible Church,'[1] fully concurs with Bunyan, as does also Dr. John Owen, in his 'Nature of a Gospel Church,' excepting that he is silent as to female deacons. Let every church be thus affectionately and scripturally governed, and in their works of faith and labours of love they will become terrible to the enemy 'as an army with banners' (Cant 6:4).

At the present day, great laxity of discipline has crept in. Some offices have been discontinued, others altered, and it becomes us most solemnly to judge ourselves by the unerring word of the living God, whether we have deviated from the order recorded by the Holy Ghost, and if so, to repent and return to the scriptural model.

GEO. OFFOR

A DISCOURSE OF THE BUILDING, &c., OF THE HOUSE OF GOD

I

BY WHOM THIS HOUSE IS BUILT

The builder's God, materials his Elect;
His Son's the rock on which it is erect;
The Scripture is his rule, plummet, or line,
Which gives proportion to this house divine,
His working-tools his ordinances are,
By them he doth his stones and timber square,
Affections knit in love, the couplings are;
Good doctrine like to mortar doth cement
The whole together, schism to prevent:
His compass, his decree; his hand's the Spirit
By which he frames, what he means to inherit,
A holy temple, which shall far excel

That very place, where now the angels dwell.

Call this a temple or a house of prayer,
A palace, oracle, or spouse most fair;
Or what you will: God's love is here displayed,
And here his treasure safely up is laid;
For his own darling none can find a place,
Where he, as here, is wont to show his face.

What though some slight it, it a cottage call,
Give't the reproachful name of beggar's hall;
Yea, what though to some it an eyesore is,
What though they count it base, and at it hiss,
Call it an alms-house, builded for the poor;
Yet kings of old have begged at the door.

II

OF THE BEAUTY OF THE CHURCH

Lo her foundations laid with sapphires are;
Her goodly windows made of agates fair,
Her gates are carbuncles, or pearls; nor one
Of all her borders but's a precious stone;
None common, nor o' th' baser sort are here,
Nor rough, but squar'd and polish'd everywhere;
Her beams are cedars, fir her rafters be,
Her terraces are of the algum-tree;
The thorn or crab-tree here are not of us;
Who thinks them here utensils, puts abuse
Upon the place, yea, on the builder too;
Would they be thus controll'd in what they do?
With carved-work of lily, and palm-tree,
With cherubims and chains adorned be
The doors, the walls, and pillars of this place;
Forbidden beasts here must not show their face.
With grace like gold, as with fine painting, he
Will have this house within enriched be;
Fig-leaves nor rags, must here keep out no cold,
This builder covers all with cloth of gold,
Of needle-work prick'd more than once or twice
(The oft'ner prick'd, still of the higher price)
Wrought by his SON, put on her by his merit,
Applied by faith, revealed by the Spirit.

III

OF THE CONVENIENCES OF THIS HOUSE

Within these walls the builder did devise
That there the householders might sacrifice;
Here is an altar, and a laver too,
And priests abundance, temple work to do;
Nor want they living offerings, nor yet fire,
Nor holy garments; what divine desire
Commands, it has bestowed on this place;
Here be the censors, here's the throne of grace;
None of the householders need go elsewhere,
To offer incense, or good news to hear.

A throne for judgment he did here erect,
Virtue to cherish, folly to detect;
Statutes and laws, unto this house he gave,
To teach who to condemn, and who to save:
By things thus wholesome taught is every brother
To fear his God, and to love one another.

And now for pleasure, solace, recreation,
Here's such as helpeth forward man's salvation.
Equal to these none can be found elsewhere,
All else turn to profuseness, sin, and care.
So situate it is, so roomy, fair,
So warm, so blessed, with such wholesome air,
That 'tis enticing: whoso wishes well
To his soul's health, should covet here to dwell.
Here's necessaries, and what will delight
The godly ear, the palate, with the sight
Of each degree and sex; here's everything
To please a beggar, and delight a king.
Chambers and galleries, he did invent,
Both for a prospect and a retirement.
For such as unto music do incline,
Here are both harps and psalteries divine:
Her cellars and banqueting-house have been,
In former days, a palace for a queen.
O house! what title to thee can be given,
So fit as that which men do give to heaven!

IV

OF THE STRENGTH AND DEFENCE OF THIS HOUSE

This house, you may be sure, will always stand;
She's builded on a rock, not on the sand;
Storms, rain, yea floods have oft upon her beat,
Yet stands she, here's a proof she is no cheat;
Fear not therefore in her for to abide,
She keeps her ground, come weather, wind or tide.
Her corner-stone has many times been try'd,

But never could the scorn, or rage, or pride,
Of all her foes, by what force they could make,
Destroy her battlements, or ground-work shake.
Here's God the Lord encamping round about
His dwelling place; nor ought we once to doubt
But that he as a watchman succour will
Those that do dwell upon his holy hill.
A wall of fire about her I will be,
And glory in the midst of her, and she
Shall be the place where I my name record;
Here I will come and bless you, saith the Lord.

The holy watchers at her gates do stand,
With their destroying weapons in their hand,
Those to defend, that in this house do dwell,
From all her enemies in earth and hell;
Safety! where is it, if it is not here?
God dwelleth in her, doth for her appear,
To help her early, and her foes confound,
And unto her will make his grace abound;
Safety is here, and also that advance,[2]
Will make a beggar sing, a cripple dance.

V

THE DELICATENESS OF THE SITUATION OF THIS HOUSE

As her foundation and her beauty's much;
Conveniences, and her defences such
As none can parallel, so doth the field
About her richest, rarest dainties yield.
Moriah, where Isaac was offered,
Where David from his sin was ransomed;
Where Solomon the temple did erect,
Compar'd with this is worthy no respect.
Under the very threshold of this place
Arise those goodly springs of lasting grace,
Whose crystal streams minister like to those
That here of love to her, make their repose.
Sweet is her aid, (as one may well infer)
'Cause 'tis the breathings of the comforter.
The pomegranates at all her gates do grow,
Mandrakes and vines, with other dainties mo;[3]
Her gardens yield the chief, the richest spice,
Surpassing them of Adam's paradise:
Here be sweet ointments, and the best of gums;
Here runs the milk, here drops the honey-combs.
Here are perfumes most pleasant to the sense,
Here grows the goodly trees of frankincense;
Her arbours, walks, fountains, and pleasant springs,

Delightful formerly have been to kings.

Such mountains round about this house do stand
As one from thence may see the holy land.
Her fields are fertile, do abound with corn;
The lilies fair, her vallies do adorn.
The birds that do come hither every spring,
For birds, they are the very best that sing.
Her friends, her neighbours too, do call her blest;
Angels do here go by, turn in and rest.
The road to paradise lies by her gate,
Here pilgrims do themselves accommodate
With bed and board, and do such stories tell
As do for truth and profit all excel.
Nor doth the porter here say any nay,
That hither would turn in, that there would stay.
This house is rent-free; here the man may dwell
That loves his landlord, rules his passions well.

VI

THE WAY OF RECEIVING THOSE THAT WOULD HERE INHABIT

And wouldst thou know the customs of this place,
How men are here admitted to this grace;
And consequently whether thou mayst be
Made one of this most blest fraternity?
Come hither then, unto me lend an ear;
And what is doubtful to thee, I will clear.

I
This place, as mercy's arms, stands ope to those
That their own happiness us'd to oppose;
Those under hedges, high-way men, or they
That would not God, nor yet good men obey;
Those that among the bushes us'd to browse,
Or under hedges us'd themselves to louze.
The vilest men, of sinners who are chief,
A fornicator, liar, or a thief,
May turn in hither, here take up and dwell
With those who ransom'd are from death and hell.

II
This place, as hospitals, will entertain,
Those which the lofty of this world disdain:
The poor, the lame, the maimed, halt and blind,
The leprous, and possessed too, may find
Free welcome here, as also such relief
As ease them will of trouble, pain and grief.

III
This place, as David's heart, with free consent
Opens to th' distressed, and the discontent;
Who is in debt, that has not wherewithal
To quit his scores, may here be free from thrall:
That man that fears the bailiff, or the jail,
May find one here that will become his bail.

IV
Art thou bound over to the great assize,
For heark'ning to the devil and his lies;
Art thou afraid thereat to shew thy head,
For fear thou then be sent unto the dead?
Thou may'st come hither, here is room and place,
For such as willingly would live by grace.

V
This place, as father's house in former days,
Is a receptacle for runaways;[4]
He that, like to the ox,[5] backslidden is,
Forfeited hath for sin his share of bliss;
May yet come hither, here is room and rest;
Of old such have come hither and been blest.
Had this been false, O woe had been to David!
Nor Peter had, nor Magdalen, been saved.
Nor Jonah, nor Manasseh, nor the rest;
No runaway from God could been blest
With kind reception at his hands; return
Would here come too late, if nought but burn
Had been the lot of the backsliding man:
But we are told there's no rebellion can
Prevent, or hinder him from being saved,
That mercy heartily of God hath crav'd.
She that went from her God to play the whore,
Returning may be as she was before:
He that refuses to his God to turn,
That is resolved in hell fire to burn;
If he bethinks himself, and turns again,
May find them here that will him entertain.

VI
But bring thou with thee a certificate,
To show thou seest thyself most desolate;
Writ by the master, with repentance seal'd,
To shew also that here thou would'st be heal'd,
By those fair leaves of that most blessed tree,
By which alone poor sinners healed be;
And that thou dost abhor thee for thy ways.
And wouldst in holiness spend all thy days;
And here be entertained; or thou wilt find
To entertain thee here are none inclin'd.[6]

VII

OF THE GOVERNORS OF THIS HOUSE

The governors that here in office are,
Such be as service do with love and care;
Not swerving from the rule, nor yet intrude
Upon each other's work, nor are they rude
In managing their own: but to their trust
They labour to be honest, faithful, just.

The chief is he who is the Lord of all,
The Saviour; some him physician call.
He's cloth'd in shining raiment to the ground,
A golden girdle doth begirt him round;
His head and hairs are white as any snow,
His eyes are like a flame of fire also;
His feet are like fine brass, as if they burn'd
Within a furnace, or to fire were turn'd;
His voice doth like to many waters sound;
In his right hand, seven glittering stars are found.
Out of his mouth goes a two-edged sword,
Sharper than any ('tis his holy word)

And for his countenance, 'tis as the sun
Which shineth in its strength, till day is done.
His name is call'd holy, The WORD OF GOD;
The wine-press of his father's wrath he trod;
At all the power of sin he doth deride,
The keys of hell and death hang at his side.
This is our governor, this is the chief,
From this physician comes our soul's relief.
He is the tree of life and hidden manna;
'Tis he to whom the children sing hosanna.
The white stone he doth give with a new name;
In heaven and earth he is of worthy fame.
This man hath death destroy'd and slain the devil,
And doth secure all his from damning evil.
He is the prince of life, the prince of peace;
He doth us from the bonds of death release.
His work is properly his own; nor may,
In what he doth, another say him nay.

'Tis he who pays our hospitalian scores,
He's here to search, supple, and bind up sores;
He is our plaster-maker, he applies
Them to our wounds, he wipes our wetted eyes.
'Tis he that gives us cups of consolation,
'Tis he renews the hopes of our salvation.

He'll take our parts, oft times to us unknown,
And make as if our failings were his own;
He'll plead with God his name and doings too,
And save us will, from those would us undo.

His name is as an ointment poured forth;
'Tis sweet from east to west, from south to north.
He's white and ruddy; yea of all the chief;
His golden head is rich beyond belief.
His eyes are like the doves which waters wet,
Well wash'd with milk, and also fitly set,
His cheeks as beds of spices, and sweet flowers.
He us'd to water with those crystal showers,
Which often flowed from his cloudy eyes;
Better by far than what comes from the skies.
His lips like lilies, drop sweet-smelling myrrh,
Scenting as do those of the comforter.
His hands are as gold rings set with the beryls;
By them we are delivered out of perils;
His legs like marble, stand in boots of gold,
His countenance is ex'lent to behold.
His mouth, it is of all a mouth most sweet,
O kiss me then, Lord, every time we meet!
Thy sugar'd lips, Lord, let them sweeten mine,
With the most blessed scent of things divine.

This is one Governor; and next in place,
One call'd the Ghost, in Honour and in Grace
No whit inferior to him; and HE
Will also in this house our helper be,
He 'twas who did at first brood the creation;
And he's the cause of man's regeneration.
'Tis he by whom the heavens were garnished,
With all their host they then abroad did spread
(Like spangles, pearls, diamonds or richest gems)
Far richer than the fairest diadems.
'Twas he who with his cloven tongues of fire
Made all those wise ones of the world admire,
Who heard his breathing in unlearned men.
O blessed ruler! now the same as then!
His work our mind is to illuminate
With things divine, and to accommodate
Us with those graces, which will us adorn,
And make us look like men indeed new-born.
For our inheritance he makes us meet;
He makes us also in this world discreet.
Prudent and wise in what we take in hand,
To do and suffer at our Lord's command.
'Tis he that leads us to the tomb and cross,
Where Jesus crucified and buried was;
He shews us also, that he did revive,

And doth assure us that he is alive;
And doth improve the merit of his blood,
At grace's throne for our eternal good.
Dark riddles he doth here to us unfold,
Yea, makes us things invisible behold.
He sheds abroad God's love in every heart,
Where he doth dwell, yea to them doth impart,
Such tokens of a future happiness,
That's past the tongue of angels to express.
'Tis he which helpeth us, that to perform,
Whether becalm'd, or whether in a storm,
Which God commands: without him we do nought
That's good, either in deed, or word, or thought.

'Tis he that doth with jewels us bedeck,
'Tis he puts chains of gold about our neck;
'Tis he that doth us with fine linen gird,
That maketh us ofttimes live as a bird.
That cureth us of all our doubts and fears,
Puts bracelets on our hands, rings on our ears;
He sanctifies our persons, he perfumes
Our spirits also; he our lust consumes;
Our stinking breath he sweetens, so that we
To God and all good men sweet-scented be;
He sets God's mark upon us, and doth seal
Us unto life, and life to us reveal.

VIII

UNDER OFFICERS

Another sort of officers here are,
But such as must not with these first compare;
They're under-officers, but serviceable,
Not only here to rule, but wait at table.
Those clothed are with linen, fine and white,
They glitter as the stars of darksome night.
They have Saint Peter's keys, and Aaron's rod;
They ope and shut, they bind and loose for God.
The chief of these are watchmen, they have power
To mount on high and to ascend the tower
Of this brave fabric, and from thence to see
Who keeps their ground, and who the stragglers be.
These have their trumpet, when they do it sound
The mountains echo, yea it shakes the ground.
With it they also sound out an alarm,
When they perceive the least mischief or harm
Is coming, so they do this house secure
There from, or else prepare it to endure
Most manfully the cross, and so attain

The crown which for the victor doth remain.

This officer is call'd a steward too,
'Cause with his master's cash he has to do,
And has authority it to disburse
To those that want, or for that treasure thirst.
The distributor of the word of grace
He is, and at his mouth, when he's in place,
They seek the law, he also bids them do it;
He shews them sin, and learns them to eschew it.
By this example too he shews them how
To keep their garments clean, their knees to bow
Before the king, when he comes into place;
And when they do him supplicate for grace.

Another bade this officer doth wear,
Is that of overseer; because the care
Of the whole house is with him, he's to see
They nothing want, nor yet abused be
By false intruders, doctrines, or (perchance)
By the misplacing of an ordinance.[7]
These also are to see they wander not
From place or duty, lest they get a blot
To their profession, or bring some disease
Upon the whole, or get a trick to lease,
Or lie unto their God, by doing what
By sacred statutes he commanded not.
Call them your cooks, they're skill'd in dressing food
To nourish weak, and strong, and cleanse the blood:
They've milk for babes, strong meat for men of age;
Food fit for who are simple, who are sage,
When the great pot goes on, as oft it doth,
They put not coloquintida[8] in broth,
As do those younglings, fondlings of their skill,
Who make not what's so apt to cure as kill.

They are your sub-physicians, and know
What sickness you are incident unto;
Let them but feel your pulse, and they will tell
You quickly whether you are sick or well.
Have you the staggers? They can help you there;
Or if the falling-sickness, or do fear
A lethargy, a fever, or the gout,
God blessing of their skill, you need not doubt
A cure, for long experience has made
These officers the masters of their trade.[9]
Their physic works by purge and vomit too,
Fear not, nor full nor fasting but 'twill do,
Have but a care, and see you catch no cold,
And with their physic then you may be bold.

You may them Prophets call, for they can tell
Of things to come, yea, here they do excel.
They prophesy of man's future event,
Whether to weal or woe his mind is bent,
Yea, so expert are they in their predictions,
Their arguments so full are of convictions,
That none who hear them, but are forced to say,
Woe unto them who wander from the way.
Art bound for hell against all wind and weather?
Or art thou one a going backward thither?
Or dost thou wink, because thou would'st not see?
Or dost thou sideling go, and would'st not be
Suspected? Yet these prophets can thee tell,
Which way thou art a going down to hell.
For him that would eternal life attain,
Yet will not part with all, that life to gain,
But keepeth some thing close, he should forsake,
Or slips the time, in which he should awake;
Or saith he lets go all, yet keepeth some
Of what will make him lose the world to come.
These prophets can tell such a man his state,
And what at last will surely be his fate.
If thou art one who tradeth in both ways,
God's now, the devil's then; or if delays
Thou mak'st of coming to thy God for life;
Or if thy light, and lusts are at a strife
About who should be master of thy soul,
And lovest one, the other dost control;
These prophets tell thee can, which way thou bendest,
On which thou frown'st, to which a hand thou lendest.
Art one of those whose fears do go beyond
Their faith? when thou should'st hope, dost thou despond?
Dost keep thine eye upon what thou hast done,
And yet hast licence to look on the sun?
Dost thou so covet more, as not to be
Affected with the grace bestowed on thee?
Art like to him, that needs must step a mile
At every stride, or think it not worth while
To follow Christ? These prophets they can tell
To cure this thy disease, and make thee well.

This officer is also call'd a guide,
Nor should the people but keep by his side;
Or tread his steps in all the paths they walk,
By his example they should do and talk.
He is to be to them instead of eyes,
He must before them go in any wise;
And he must lead them by the water side,
This is the work of this our Faithful Guide.
Since snares, and traps, and gins are for us set,
Since here's a hole, and there is spread a net,

O let no body at my muse deride,
No man can travel here without a guide.
Here's tempting apples, here are baited hooks,
With turning, twisting, cramping, tangling crooks
Close by the way; woe then to them betide,
That dare to venture here without a guide.
Here haunt the fairies with their chanting voice;
Fiends like to angels, to bewitch our choices;
Baits for the flesh lie here on every side:
Who dares set here one foot without a guide
Master delusion dwelleth by our walks,
Who with confusion, sings and prays and talks;
He says the straight path's his, and ours the wide:
What then can we do here without a guide
Let God then give our leaders always eyes;
Yea, let him make them holy, bold, and wise;
And help us fast by them for to abide,
And suffer not the blind to be our guide.[10]

Here are of rulers, yet another sort,
Such as direct our manners to comport
With our professed faith, that we to view,
May let beholders know that we are new.
These are our conversations to inspect,
And us in our employments to direct,
That we in faith and love do every thing,
That reacheth from the peasant to the king.
That there may be no scandal in our ways,
Nor yet in our profession all our days.
These should after our busy-bodies look,
Tale-bearers also, they have undertook
To keep in order, also they must see
None that can work among us idle be;
Jars, discords, frauds, with grievances and wrongs,
These they're to regulate; to them belongs
The judgment of all matters of this kind,
And happy is the house thus disciplined.

Another sort of officers we have,
Deacons we call them 'cause their work's to save
And distribute those crumbs of charity
Unto the poor, for their subsistency,
That contributed is for their relief,
Which of their bus'ness is indeed the chief.
These must be grave, not of a double tongue,
Not given to wine, not apt to do a wrong
Unto the poor, through love to lucre. (Just
In this their office, faithful to their trust)
The wife must answer here as face doth face;
The husband's fitness to his work and place,
That ground of scandal or of jealousy

Obstructs not proof that he most zealously
Performs his office well, for then shall he
Be bold in faith, and get a good degree
Of credit with the church; yea what is more,
He shall possess the blessings of the poor.
His wisdom teach him will, to find out who
Is poor of idleness, and who comes to
A low estate by sickness, age, or 'cause
The want of limbs, or sight, or work it was
That brought them to it; or such destiny
As sometimes maketh low, who once were high.
They must remember too, that some there are
Who halt before they're lame, while others care
Not to make known their want, they'll rather die,
Than charge the churches with their poverty.
This done, they must bestow as they see cause;
Making the word the rule, and want the laws
By which they act, and then they need not pause.
The table of the Lord, he also must
Provide for, 'tis his duty and his trust.
The teacher too should have his table spread
By him; thus should his house be clad and fed;
Thus he serves tables with the church's stock,
And so becomes a blessing to the flock.[11]

I read of widows also that should be
Employed here for further decency;
I dare not say they are in office, though
A service here they are appointed to:
They must be very aged, trusty, meek,
Such who have done much good, that do not seek
Themselves; they must be humble, pitiful,
Or they will make their service void and null.
These are to teach the younger women what
Is proper to their sex and state, what not:
To be discreet, keepers at home, and chaste;
To love their husbands, to be good; shamefac'd:
Children to bear, to love them, and to fly
What to the gospel would be infamy.
I think those to the sick should look also,
A work unfit for younger ones to do.
Wherefore he saith, The younger ones refuse;
Perhaps because their weakness would abuse
Them, and subject them unto great disgrace,
When such a one as Amnon is in place.
And since the good old woman this must do
'Tis fit she should be fed and clothed too,
Out of the deacon's purse, let it so be;
And let this be her service constantly.[12]

THE ORDER AND MANNER OF THE GOVERNMENT HERE

As I have shew'd you who in office are,
So I will tell you how, and with what care
Those here intrusted with the government,
Keep to the statutes made to that intent.
By rules divine this house is governed;
Not sanguinary ones, nor taught nor fed
By human precepts: for the scripture saith,
The word's our ghostly food; food for our faith.
Nor are all forced to the same degree
In things divine, tho' all exhorted be
To the most absolute proficiency
That law or duty can to them descry.

Alas! here's children, here are great with young;
Here are the sick and weak, as well as strong.
Here are the cedar, shrub, and bruised reed;
Yea, here are such who wounded are, and bleed.
As here are some who in their grammar be,
So here are others in their A, B, C.
Some apt to teach, and others hard to learn;
Some see far off, others can scarce discern
That which is set before them in the glass;
Others forgetful are, and so let pass,
Or slip out of their mind what they did hear
But now; so great our differences appear
Wherefore our Jacob's must have special care
They drive their flocks, but as their flocks can bear;
For if they be o'erdriven, presently
They will be sick, or cast their young, or die.
The laws therefore are more and less of force,
According as they bring us to the source,
Or head, or fountain, or are more remote
To what at first we should ourselves devote.
Be we then wise in handling of the laws,
Not making a confused noise like daws
In chambers, yea let us seek to excel,
To each man's profit; this is ruling well.
With fundamentals then let us begin,
For they strike at the very root of sin.
So the foundation being strongly laid,
Let us go on, as the wise builder said,
For I don't mean, we should at all disdain
Those that are less, we always should maintain
That due respect to either which is meet;
This is the way to sit at Jesus' feet.

Repent I must, or I am cast away;

Believe I must, or nothing I obey:
Love God I must, or nothing I can do,
That's worth so much as loosing of my shoe.
If I do not, bear after Christ, my cross;
If love to holiness is at a loss;
If I my lusts seek not to mortify;
If to myself, my flesh, I do not die;
What law, should I observe't, can do me good?
In little duties life hath never stood.

One reads, he prays, he catechises too;
But doth he nothing else, what doth he do?
I read to know my duty, I do pray
To God to help me do it day by day;
If this be not my end in what I do,
I am a sot, an hypocrite also.
I am baptiz'd, what then? unless I die
To sin, I cover folly with a lie.
At the Lord's table, I do eat; what though?
There some have eat their own damnation too.

I will suppose, I hear, I sing, I pray,
And that I am baptiz'd without delay,
I will suppose I do much knowledge get,
And will also suppose that I am fit
To be a preacher, yet nought profits me
If to the first, poor I a stranger be:
They are more weighty therefore; in compare
These unto them, but mint and anise are.

Not that I would the least of duty slight,
Because the least command, of divine right,
Requires that I myself subject thereto;
Willful resisters do themselves undo.
But let's keep order, let the first be first;
Repent, believe, and love; and then I trust
I have that right, which is divine, to all
That is enjoined; be they great or small.
Only I must as cautionary speak,
In one word more, a little to the weak;
Thou must not suffer men so to enclose
Thee in their judgments, as to discompose
Thee in that faith and peace thou hast with him;
This would be like the losing of a limb;
Or like to him who thinks he doth not well,
Unless he lose the kernel for the shell.
Thou art no captive, but a child and free;
Thou wast not made for laws, but laws for thee;
And thou must use them as thy light will bear it;
They that say otherwise, do rend and tear it,
More like to wicked tyrants, who are cruel,

And add unto a little fire, more fuel.
But those who are true shepherds of the sheep,
To quench such burnings would most gladly weep.
But I am yet but upon generals;
Particulars our legislator calls
For at our hands, and that in order to
Consummate what we have begun to do.

I.

My brother I must love, in very deed.
I'm taught of God to do it: let me heed
This divine duty, and perform it well,
Who loves his brother, God in him doth dwell;
The argument which on me this imposes,
Smells like to ointment, or the sweetest roses.
Shall God love, shall he keep his faith to me?
And shall not I? shall I unfaithful be?
Shall God love me a sinner? and shall I
Not love a saint? Yea, shall my Jesus die
To reconcile me to my God? and shall
I hate his child, nor hear his wants that call
For my little assisting of him? fie
On such a spirit, on such cruelty;
Fie on the thought that would me alienate,
Or tempt me my worst enemy to hate.[13]

II.

He that dwells here, must also be a sharer
In others' griefs; must be a burden-bearer
Among his brethren, or he cannot do
That which the blessed gospel calls him to.
In order hereunto, humility
Must be put on, it is our livery,
We must be clothed with it, if we will
The law obey, our master's mind fulfil.
If this be so, then what should they do here,
Who in their antic pranks of pride appear?
Let lofty men among you bear no sway,
The Lord beholds the proud man far away.
It is not fit that he inhabit there
Where humbleness of mind should have the chair.
Can pride be where a soul for mercy craves?
Shall pride be found among redeemed slaves?
Shall he who mercy from the gallows brought,
Look high, or strut, or entertain a thought
That tends to tempt him to forget that fate,
To which for sin he destin'd was of late,
And could not then at all delivered be,
But by another's death and misery?
Pride is the unbecoming'st thing of all:
Besides, 'tis the forerunner of a fall.

He that is proud, soon in the dirt will lie,
But honour followeth humility.
Let each then count his brother as his better,
Let each esteem himself another's debtor.
Christ bids us learn of him, humble to be,
Profession's beauty is humility.

III.
Forgive, is here another statute law;
To be revenged is not worth a straw,
He that forgives shall also be forgiven,
Who doth not so, must lose his part in heaven;
Nor must thou weary of this duty be
'Cause God's not weary of forgiving thee.

Thou livest by forgiveness; should a stop
Be put thereto one moment, thou wouldst drop
Into the mouth of hell. Then let this move
Thee thy dear brother to forgive in love.

And we are bid in our forgivenesses
To do as God doth in forgiving his.
If any have a quarrel against any,
(As quarrels we have oft against a many)
Why then, as God, for Christ's sake, pardons you,
For Christ's sake, pardon thou thy brother too.
We say, What freely comes, doth freely go;
Then let all our forgivenesses be so.
I'm sure God heartily forgiveth thee,
My loving brother, prithee forgive me;
But then in thy forgiveness be upright;
Do't with thine heart, or thou'rt an hypocrite.

IV.
As we forgive, so we must watch and pray;
For enemies we have, that night and day,
Should we not watch, would soon our graces spoil,
Should we not pray, would our poor souls defile.
Without a watch, resist a foe who can?
Who prays not, is not like to play the man?
Complaint that he is overcome, he may;
But who would win the field, must watch and pray.
Who watches, should know who and who's together:
Know we not friends from foes, how know we whether
Of them to fight, or which to entertain?
Some have instead of foes, familiars slain.
Sometimes a lust will get into the place,
Or work, or office, of some worthy grace;
Till it has brought our souls to great decay.
Unless we diligently watch and pray,
Our pride will our humility precede:

By th' nose, our unbelief our faith will lead.
Self-love will be where self-denial should;
And passion heat, what patience sometime cool'd.
And thus it will be with us night and day,
Unless we diligently watch and pray.

Besides what these domestics do, there are
Abroad such foes as wait us to ensnare;
Yea, they against us stand in battle-'ray,
And will us spoil, unless we watch and pray.
There is the world with all its vanities,
There is the devil with a thousand lies;
There are false brethren with their fair collusions,
Also false doctrines with their strong delusions;
These will us take, yea carry us away
From what is good, unless we watch and pray.
Long life to many, is a fearful snare;
Of sudden death we also need beware;
The smiles and frowns of men, temptations be;
And there's a bait in all we hear and see.
Let them who can, to any shew a way,
How they should live, that cannot watch and pray.

Nor is't enough to keep all well within,
Nor yet to keep all out that would be sin,
If entertained; I must myself concern
With my dear brother, as I do discern
Him tempted, or a wand'ring from the way;
Else as I should, I do not watch and pray.
Pray then, and watch, be thou no drowsy sleeper,
Grudge, nor refuse, to be thy brother's keeper,
Seest thou thy brother's graces at an ebb?
Is his heel taken in the spider's web?
Pray for thy brother; if that will not do,
To him, and warn him of the present woe
That is upon him; if he shall thee hear
Thou wilt a saviour unto him appear.[14]

V.
Sincerity, to that we are enjoined,
For I do in our blessed law-book find,
That duties, how well done soe'er they seem,
With our great God, are but of small esteem
If not sincerely done; then have a care
For hypocrites are hateful everywhere.
Things we may do, yea, and may let men see
Us do them too, design but honestly;
Vain-gloriously let us not seek for praise,
Vain-glory's nothing worth in gospel days.
Sincerity seeks not an open place,
To do, tho' it does all with open face;

It loves no guises, nor disfigurations.
'Tis plain, 'tis simple, hates equivocations.
Sincerity's that grace by which we poise,
And keep our duties even: nor but toys
Are all we do, if no sincerity
Attend our works, lift it up ne'er so high.
Sincerity makes heav'n upon us smile,
Lo, here's a man in whom there is no guile!
Nathaniel, an Israelite indeed!'
With duties he sincerely doth proceed;
Under the fig-tree heav'n saw him at prayer,
There is but few do their devotions there.
Sincerity! Grace is thereto entailed,
The man that was sincere, God never fail'd.
One tear that falleth from sincerity,
Is worth ten thousand from hypocrisy.

VI.
Meekness is also here imposed by law,
A froward spirit is not worth a straw.
A froward spirit is a bane to rest,
They find it so, who lodge it in their breast.
A froward spirit suits with self-denial,
With taking up the cross, and ev'ry trial,
As cats and dogs, together by the ears;
As scornful men do suit with frumps[15] and jeers.
Meek as a lamb, mute as a fish, is brave,
When anger boils, and passions vent do crave.
The meek, God will in paths of judgment guide;
Good shall the meek eat, and be satisfied;
The Lord will lift the meek to highest station;
Will beautify the meek with his salvation.
The meek are blest, the earth they shall inherit:
The meek is better than the proud in spirit.
Meekness will make you quiet, hardy, strong,
To bear a burden, and to put up wrong.
Meekness, though divers troubles you are in,
Will bridle passion, be a curb to sin.
Thus God sets forth the meek before our eyes;
A meek and quiet spirit God doth prize.

VII.
Temp'rance also, is on this house imposed,
And whoso has it not, is greatly nosed[16]
By standers by, for greedy, lustful men:
Nor can all we can say, excuse us, when
Intemp'rance any where to them shall be
Apparent; though we other vices flee.
Temperance, the mother is of moderation,
The beauty also of our conversation.
Temperance will our affections moderate,

And keep us from being inordinate
In our embraces, or in our salutes
Of what we have, also in our pursuits
Of more, and in a sedate settlement
Of mind, will make's in all states be content.
Nor want we here an argument to prove
That who, inordinate is, in his love
Of worldly things, doth better things defy,
And slight salvation for the butterfly.

What argument can any man produce,
Why we should be intemperate in the use
Of any worldly good? Do we not see
That all these things from us a fleeting be?
What can we hold? What can we keep from flying
From us? Is not each thing we have a dying?
My house, my wife, my child, they all grow old,
Nor am I e'er the younger for my gold;
Here's none abiding, all things fade away,
Poor I at best am but a clod of clay.

If that be true, man doth not live by bread,
He that has nothing else, must needs be dead;
Take bread for what can in this world be found,
Yet all that therein is, is but a sound,
An empty sound, there is no life at all,
It cannot save a sparrow from her fall.
Let us then use this world as we are bid,
And as in olden times, the godly did.
Who buy, should be as if they did possess
None of their purchase, or themselves did bless
In what they have; and he that doth rejoice
In what he hath, should rather out of choice,
Withdraw his mind from what he hath below,
And set his heart on whither he must go.
For those that weep under their heavy crosses,
Or that are broken with the sense of losses,
Let them remember, all things here are fading,
And as to nature, of a self-degrading
And wasting temper; yea, both we and they
Shall waste, and waste, until we waste away.
Let temperance then, with moderation be
As bounds to our affections, when we see,
Or feel, or taste, or any ways enjoy
Things pleasing to the flesh, lest we destroy
Ourselves therewith, or bring ourselves thereby
To surfeits, guilt, or Satan's slavery.

VIII.
Patience, another duty, as we find
In holy writ, is on this house enjoined;

Her state, while here, is such, that she must have
This grace abounding in her, or a slave
She'll quickly be unto their lusts and will,
That seek the mind of Satan to fulfil.
He who must bear all wrongs without resistance,
And that with gladness too, must have assistance
Continually from patience, thereunto,
Or he will find such work too hard to do.
Who meets with taunts, with mocks, with flouts and squibs,
With raileries, reproaches, checks, and snibs;
Yea, he who for well-doing is abused,
Robb'd, spoiled, and goal'd, and ev'ry way misused;
Has he not patience soon will be offended,
Yea his profession too will soon be ended.
A Christian for religion must not fight,
But put up wrongs, though he be in the right;
He must be merciful, loving, and meek,
When they smite one, must turn the other cheek.
He must not render railing for reviling
Nor murmur when he sees himself a spoiling,
When they shall curse, he must be sure to bless,
And thus with patience must his soul possess.
I doubt our frampered[17] Christians will not down
With what I say, yet I dare pawn my gown,
Do but compare my notes with sacred story,
And you will find patience the way to glory.
Patience under the cross, a duty is,
Whoso possess it, belongs to bliss;
If it is present work accomplisheth;
If it holds out, and still abideth with
The Truth; then may we look for that reward,
Promised at the coming of the Lord.

IX.
To entertain good men let's not forget
Some by so doing have had benefit;
Yea for to recompense this act of theirs,
Angels have lodged with them unawares.
Yea to encourage such a work as this,
The Lord himself makes it a note of his,
When hungry or when thirsty I have been,
Or when a stranger, you did take me in.
Strangers should not to strangers but be kind
Specially if conferring notes, they find
Themselves, though strangers here, one brotherhood,
And heirs, joint heirs, of everlasting good;
These should as mother's sons, when they do meet
In a strange country, one another greet
With welcome; come in, brother, how dost do?
Whither art wand'ring? Prithee let me know
Thy state? Dost want or meat, or drink, or cloth?

Art weary? Let me wash thy feet, I'm loth
Thou shouldst depart, abide with me all night;
Pursue thy journey with the morning light.

X

THE WAY OF REDUCING WHAT'S AMISS, INTO ORDER HERE

Although this house thus honourable is,
Yet 'tis not sinless, many things amiss
Do happen here, wherefore them to redress,
We must keep to our rules of righteousness;
Nor must we think it strange, if sin shall be
Where virtue is; don't all men plainly see
That in the holy temple there was dust,
That to our very gold, there cleaveth rust?
In Abraham's family was a derider
I' th' palace of a king will be the spider.
Who saith, we have no sin, doth also say
We have no need at all to watch and pray;
To live by faith, the flesh to mortify,
Or of more of the spirit to sanctify
Our nature. All this wholly needless is
With him, who as to this, has nought amiss.
But we confess, 'cause we would not be liars,
That we still feel the motions and desires
Of sin within us, and should fall away,
Did not Christ intercede and for us pray.
We therefore do conclude that sin is here,
But that it may not to our shame appear,
We have our rules, thereby with it to deal,
And plaisters too, our deadly wounds to heal.
And seeing idleness gives great occasions
To th' flesh, to make its rude and bold invasions
Upon good orders, 'tis ordained we see,
That none dwell here, but such as workers be:
So plain's the law for this, and so complete,
It bids who will not work, forbear to eat;
Let then each one be diligent to do
What grace or nature doth oblige them to.
Who have no need to work for meat or clothes,
Should work for those that want. Not that the sloth
Of idleness should be encouraged,
But that those, poor indeed, be clad and fed.
Dorcas did thus, and 'tis to sacred story
Committed for her praise and lasting glory.

This house then is no nurse to idleness;
Fig-trees are here to keep, and vines to dress;
Here's work for all; yea, work that must be done;

Yet work, like that, to playing in the sun;
The toil's a pleasure, and the labour sweet,
Like that of David's dancing in the street;
The work is short, the wages are for ever,
The work like me, the wages like the giver

No drone must hide himself under those eaves;
Who sows not, will in harvest reap no sheaves.
The slothful man himself, may plainly see,
That honey's gotten by the working bee.
But here's no work for life, that's freely given;
Meat, drink, and cloths, and life, we have from heav'n;
Work's here enjoined, 'cause it is a pleasure,
Vice to suppress, and augment heavenly treasure
Moreover, 'tis to shew, if men profess
The faith, and yet abide in idleness,
Their faith is vain, no man can ever prove
He's right, but by the faith that works by love.
If this good counsel is by thee rejected;
If work and labour is by thee neglected;
If thou, like David, lollest on thy bed;
Or art like to a horse, pamper'd and fed
With what will fire thy lusts, and so lay snares
For thine own soul, when thou shalt be i' th' wars:
Then take what follows, sin must be detected,
And thou without repentance quite rejected.

This is the house of God, his dwelling-place,
'Tis here that we behold his lovely face;
But if it should polluted be with sin,
And so abide, he quickly will begin
To leave it desolate, and then woe to it,
Sin and his absence quickly will undo it.

And since sin is, of things the worst of all,
And watcheth like a serpent on a wall,
Or flyeth like an eagle in the air,
Or runs as desperate ships, void of all care,
Or, (as great Solomon hath wisely said)
Is as the way of wantons with a maid,
Who tick, and toy, and with a tempting giggle
Provoke to lust, and by degrees, so wriggle
Them into their affections, that they go
The way to death, so do themselves undo:
As it is said, this mischief to prevent,
Let all men watch, yea, and be diligent
Observers of its motions, and then fly,
This is the way to live, and not to die.
He that would never fall, must never slip,
Who would obey the call, must fear the whip.
God would also that every stander by

That in the grass doth see the adder lie,
Should cry as he did, death is in the pot,
That many by its poison perish not.
But if that beastly thing shall hold its hold,
And make the man possessed basely bold
In pleading for it, or shall it deny,
Or it shall seek to cover with a lie;
Then take more aid, and make a fresh assault
At it again, diminish not the fault,
But charge it home. If yet he will not fear,
But still unto his wickedness adhere,
Then tell the house thereof. But if he still
Persist in his abomination will,
Then fly him, 'cause he is a leprous man,
Count him with heathens and the publican.
But if he falls before thee at the first,
Then be thou to him faithful, loving, just.
Forgive his sin, tell it not to a brother,
Lest thou thyself be served so by another.

If he falls not, but in the second charge,
Spread not his wickedness abroad at large.
But, if thou think his sorrow to be sound,
Forgive his sin, and hide it under ground.
If he shall stand the first and second shot;
If he before the church, repenteth not,
Deal with him as the matter shall require,
Let not the house for him be set on fire.
If after all, he shall repent and turn
To God, and you, you must not let him burn
For ever under sense of sin and shame,
You must his sin forgive in Christ his name.

Confirm your love to him in Christ, you must,
By all such ways as honest are, and just.
Shy be not of him, carry't not aloof,
But rather give him of your love such proof,
That he may gather thence, ye do believe
To mercy Christ again doth him receive.

Two things, monish you, as to this, I would;
The first, to shew the church wherein she should
In all her actions so herself behave,
As to convince the fault, she would save
His soul; and that 'tis for this very thing,
She doth him unto open judgment bring.
Then would I shew the person they reject,
What will, without repentance, be th' effect
Of this tremendous censure, so conclude;
Leaving my judgment to the multitude
Of those who sober and judicious be,

Begging of each of them a prayer for me.

I.

This house, in order to this work, must be
Affected with the sin and misery,
Of this poor creature, yea, must mourn and weep,
To think such tares, in your neglect, or sleep,
Should spring up here, nor must they once invent
To think, till he's cast out, you're innocent.

II.

Thus leaven, the whole lump has leavened;
Israel was guilty of what Achan did;
And so must stand, until they purged are,
Till Achan doth, for sin, his burden bear.
The reason is, Achan a member was
Of that great body, and by nature's laws,
The hand, foot, eye, tongue, ear, or one of these,
May taint the whole with Achan's foul disease.
The church must too be sensible of this,
Some lep'rous stones make all the house amiss:
And as the stones must thence removed be,
In order to the house's sanctity,
So it must purged be (in any wise)
Before 'tis counted clean (by sacrifice).

III.

Next have a care, lest sin, which you should purge
Becomes not unto you a farther scourge,
The which it will, if such shall judges be,
Which from its spots and freckles are not free;
Pluck thou the beam first out of thine own eye,
Else the condemned will thee vilify
And say, let not the pot the kettle judge;
If otherwise, it will beget a grudge,
A great one 'twixt the church and him that sinned,
Nor by such means, can ever such be winned
To a renew'd embrace of holiness;
More like be tempted further to transgress.

IV.

Again, let those that loud against it cry,
See they don't entertain it inwardly;
Sin, like to pitch, will to the fingers cleave,
Look to it then, let none himself deceive;
'Tis catching; make resistances afresh,
Abhor the garment spotted by the flesh.
Some at the dimness of the candle puff,
Who yet can daub their fingers with the snuff.

V.

Beware, likewise, lest rancour should appear
Against the person, do in all things fear:
Bewail the man, while you abhor his sin;
Pity his soul; the flesh you still are in;
Thyself consider thou may'st tempted be,
Hast thou no pity, who will pity thee?

VI.
See that the ground be good on which you go:
Sin, but not virtue show dislike unto.
Take heed of hypocritical intentions,
And quarrel not at various apprehensions
About some smaller matter, lest it breed
Needless debates, and lest that filthy seed
Contention, should o'errun your holy ground,
And lest not love, but nettles there are found.

VII.
You must likewise allow each man his grains,
For that none perfect are, sin yet remains,
And human frailties do attend the best;
To bear and forbear here, will tend to rest.
Vain jangling, jars, and strifes will there abound,
Where moles are mountains made, or fault is found,
With every little, trivial, petty thing;
This spirit snib, or 'twill much mischief bring
Into this house, and 'tis for want of love,
'Tis entertain'd: it is not of the dove.

VIII.
For those that have private opinions too
We must make room, or shall the church undo:
Provided they be such as don't impair
Faith, holiness, nor with good conscience jar:
Provided also those that hold them shall
Such faith hold to themselves, and not let fall
Their fruitless notions in their brother's way,
Do this, and faith and love will not decay.

IX.
We must also in these our dealings shew
We put a difference 'twixt those sins that do
Clash with the light of nature, and what we
Perceive against the faith of Christ to be.
Those against nature, nature will detect;
Those against faith, faith from them must direct
The judgment, conscience, understanding too,
Or there will be no cure, whate'er you do.
When men are caught in immoralities,
Nature will start, the conscience will arise
To judgment; and if impudence doth recoil,

Yet guilt, and self-condemnings will embroil
The wretch concerned, in such unquietness
Or shame, as will induce him to confess
His fault, and pardon crave of God and man,
Such men with ease therefore we conquer can.

But 'tis not thus with such as swerve in faith
With them, who, as our wise Apostle saith,
Entangled are at unawares, with those
Cunning to trap, to snare, and to impose
By falsifyings, their prevarications:
No, these are slyly taken from their stations,
Unknown to nature; yea, in judgment they
Think they have well done to forsake the way.
Their understanding, and their judgment too
Doth like, or well approve of what they do.
These are, poor souls, beyond their art and skill,
Ta'en captive by the devil, at his will,
Here therefore you must patience exercise,
And suffer long, ye must not tyrannize
It over such, but must all meekness shew;
Still dropping of good doctrine as the dew,
Against their error; so its churlishness
You conquer will, and may their fault redress.

The reason why we must not exercise
That roughness here, as where conviction lies
In nature, is because those thus ensnared
Want nature's light and help to be repair'd.
A spirit hath them taken, they are gone,
Delusions supernat'ral they're on
The wing of; They are out o' th' reach of man
Nothing but God, and gospel reach them can.
Now since we cannot give these people eyes,
Nor regulate their judgment, wherein lies,
Our work with them, if not, as has been said,
In exercising patience. While display'd
The holy word before their faces is,
By which alone they must see what's amiss
With their poor souls, and so convert again,
To him with whom salvation doth remain.

Obj. But they are turbulent, they would confound
The truth, and all in their perdition drown'd.

Ans. If turbulent and mischievous they are,
Imposing their opinions without care
Who they offend, or do destroy thereby.
Then must the church deal with them presently,
Lest tainted be the whole with their delusion,
And brought into disorder and confusion.

XI

THE PRESENT CONDITION OF THOSE THUS DEALT WITH

The man that worthily rejected is,
And cast out of this house, his part in bliss
Is lost for ever, turns he not again,
True faith and holiness to entertain.
Nor is it boot, for who are thus cast out,
Themselves to flatter, or to go about
To shift the censure; nothing here will do,
Except a new conversion thou come to.
He that is bound on earth, is bound in heaven,
Nor is his loosing, but the sin forgiven;
Repentance too, forgiveness must precede,
Or thou must still abide among the dead.

XII

AN EXPOSTULATION WITH SUCH TO RETURN

O shame! Is't not a shame for men to be
For sin, spu'd out from good society!
For man enlightened to be so base!
To turn his back upon the God of grace!
For one who for his sins has mourn'd and cry'd,
To slight him, who for sin hath bled and died!
What fool would sell his part in paradise,
That has a soul, and that of such a price?
What parallel can suit with such so well,
As those, for sin cast down from heaven to hell!
But let me tell thee, here is aggravation;
The angels, though they did fall from their station
Had not the caution thou hast had; they fell;
This thou hast seen, and seeing, didst rebel.
One would a thought, the noise of this their fall,
A warning; yea, a warning, and a call,
Should unto thee have been, to have a care
Of falling too: O how then didst thou dare,
Since God did not spare them, thus to presume
To tempt him in his wrath, thee to consume.
Nor did the angels from a Jesus fall,
Redeemed they were not, from a state of thrall;
But thou! as one redeem'd, and that by blood,
Redemption hast despised; and the mud
Or mire of thine own filth again embracest:
A dying bleeding Jesus thou disgracest!
What wilt thou do? see's not how thou hast trod

Under thy foot, the very Son of God?
O fearful hand of God! And fearful will
Thy doom be, when his wrath thy soul shall kill.

Yea, with a signal these must hear their sin,
This dirty sow from mire has washed been,
Yet there did wallow, after wash'd she was;
So to procure a lust, obtain'd this loss.
O shame! is't not a shame for man to be,
So much averse to his felicity,
That none can make him leave to play the fool,
Till to the devil he be put to school,
To learn his own salvation to prize?
O fool! must now the devil make thee wise?
O sot! that will in wickedness remain,
Unless the devil drives thee back again.

Hast quite forgot how thou wast wont to pray,
And cry out for forgiveness night and day?
Or dost thou count they were but painted fears
Which from thine eyes did squeeze so many tears?
Remember man, thy prayers and tears will cry
Thee down to hell, for thine apostacy.
Who will not have what he has prayed for,
Must die the death, his prayer shall him abhor.
Hast thou forgotten that most solemn vow
Thou mad'st to God, when thou didst crave he bow
His ear unto thee would, and give thee grace,
And would thee also in his arms embrace?
That vow, I say, whereby thou then didst bind
Thyself to him, that now thy roving mind
Recoil against him should, and fling away
From him, and his commandments disobey.
What has he done? wherein has he offended?
Thou actest now, as if thou wast intended
To prove him guilty of unrighteousness,
Of breach of promise, or that from distress
He could, or would not save thee, or that thou
Hast found a better good than he; but how
Thou wilt come off, or how thou wilt excuse
Thyself, 'cause thou art gone, and did refuse
To wait upon him that consider well;
Thou art as yet alive, on this side hell.
Is't not a shame, a stinking shame to be
Cast forth God's vineyard as a barren tree?
To be thrown o'er the pales, and there to lie,
Or be pick'd up by th' next that passeth by?

Well, thou hast turn'd away, return again;
Bethink thyself, thy foot from sin refrain;
Hark! thou art call'd upon, stop not thine ear:

Return, backsliding children, come, draw near
Unto your God; repent, and he will heal
Your base backslidings, to you will reveal
That grace and peace which with him doth remain,
For them that turn away, and turn again.

Take with thee words, come to the throne of grace
There supplicate thy God, and seek his face;
Like to the prodigal, confess thy sin,
Tell him where, and how vicious thou hast been.
Suppose he shall against thee shut the door,
Knock thou the louder, and cry out the more;
What if he makes thee there to stand a while?
Or makes as if he would not reconcile
To thee again? Yet take thee no denial,
Count all such carriages but as a trial
Whether thou art in earnest in thy suit,
As one truly forlorn and destitute;
But hide thou nought of all that thou hast done,
Open thy bosom, make confession
Of all thy wickedness, tell every whit;
Hast thou a secret sin? don't cover it;
Confess, thyself judge, if thou wouldst not die;
Who doth himself judge, God doth justify.

To sin, and stand in't, is the highest evil;
This makes a man most like unto the devil;
This bids defiance unto God and grace;
This man resists him spitteth in his face,
Scorns at his justice, mocketh at his power,
Tempts him, provokes him, grieves him every hour:
When he ariseth, he will recompense
This sturdy rebel for his impenitence:
Be not incorrigible then, come back again,
There's hope, beg mercy while life doth remain.

Obj. But I fear I am lost and cast away,
Sentence is past, and who reverse it may?

Ans. The sentence past, admitteth or reprieve;
Yea, of a pardon, canst thou but believe.
TURN AGAIN SINNER, NEVER MAKE A DOUBT,
COME, THE LORD JESUS WILL NOT CAST THEE OUT.

FOOTNOTES:

1. *4to, London, 1642. In the editor's library.*

2. *'That advance,' preferment, or progress towards perfection.–Ed.*

3. 'Mo,' a usual contraction for more in former times, now obsolete.–Ed.

4. Probably referring to the parable of the prodigal son, Luke 15.–Ed.

5. This may refer to the Levitical law, Exodus 21:28-36. The ox that had gored any one to death, 'shall be surely stoned' without possibility of escape, but the backslider or manslayer, although he lie equally under the sentence of death, yet may escape to the city of refuge.–Ed.

6. These stanzas afford an excellent illustration to the meaning of Bunyan in his Pilgrim's Progress, where Christian, before the cross, receives the roll or certificate–loses it for a season in the arbour on the hill Difficulty, when loitering and sleeping on his way to the Interpreter's house, but regains it by repentance and prayers, and eventually, having crossed the river, gives it in at the gate of the Celestial City, and is admitted.–Ed.

7. Bunyan considered that baptism is to follow belief, and that christening a child was a misplacing the ordinance. So also with he Lord's Supper–that it was to be a public showing forth the death of the Saviour, and if administered in private, or with any other view, it was misplaced.–Ed.

8. It is a rare thing for Bunyan to use a foreign word; but all pious persons in his time were familiar with, and generally used, the Puritan or Genevan Bible, vulgarly called the Breeches Bible, an extremely valuable book; in the marginal notes of which, on this passage is the following explanation, '"wilde gourdes," which the apoticaries call coloquintida, and is most vehement and dangerous in purging.'-Ed.

9. The university or college in which Bunyan so highly graduated, is the only one where ministers can be instructed in this spiritual physic. It is Christ's college or school, neither at Oxford or Cambridge, but in the Bible. There, and there only, under the teaching of the Holy Spirit, can the Christian bishop or under shepherd receive instruction in the precious remedies against Satan's devices, or in specifics to cure spiritual maladies.–Ed.

10. 'He had in his pocket A MAP of all ways leading to or from the celestial city; wherefore he struck a light, for he never went without his tinder box, and took a view of his book or map; which bid him be careful, in that place, to turn to the right hand way. And had he not here been careful to look in his map, they had, in all probability, been smothered in the mud; for just before them, and that in the cleanest way, was a pit, and none knows how deep, full of nothing but mud, there made on purpose to destroy pilgrims in. Then thought I with myself, who that goeth on pilgrimage, but would have one of these maps about him, that he may look when he is at a stand which is the way he must take.'–Pilgrim's Progress, Part Second.

11. These hints to deacons are invaluable. They must have been the result of long intimacy and enlightened watchfulness over the conduct of the poor. To distinguish between the noisy beggar and the unobtrusive sufferer–to administer relief in just proportions, 'the word the rule, and want the law,' in spite of all that influence which is constantly brought to bear upon those who distribute any common charity fund. It requires much of the fear of God in the heart, and a solemn sense of responsibility at the great day. The terms, 'crumbs of charity,' are beautifully expressive of the general poverty of Christian churches.–Ed.

12. Bunyan's idea of this scriptural order of female deacons is very striking, and worthy the solemn consideration of all Christian churches. They are to be chosen from such as are 'widows indeed, who trust in God, and continue in supplications and prayers night and day,' 1 Timothy 5:5. They are to

devote themselves to the sick–to be patterns of good works–and, if needful, to be fed and clothed at the expense of the church, verse 16. If to this were added to examine and educate the children, they might be most eminently useful.–Ed.

13. These instructions are like 'apples of gold in pictures of silver.' Thrice happy are those churches whose members act in conformity with these scriptural rules. But is there a member who dares to violate them? Poor wretched creature, the Lord have mercy on thee.–Ed.

14. Happy is that Christian, who, in obedience to his Lord's command, is so humble as to seek out the brother who has offended him; 'Go and tell him his fault between thee and him alone,' is the divine command. Is it not at the peril of our souls willfully to violate this self-humiliating but imperative law?–Ed.

15. To 'frump,' to mock or browbeat.–Ed.

16. 'Greatly nosed,' taken by the nose, ridiculed.–Ed.

17. 'Frampered' or frampold, peevish, crossgrained, rugged; now obsolete.–Ed.

PRISON MEDITATIONS

This poem was written in 1665, in response to a letter of encouragement Bunyan had received in prison.

Friend, I salute thee in the Lord,
And wish thou may'st abound
In faith, and have a good regard
To keep on holy ground.

Thou dost encourage me to hold
My head above the flood;
Thy counsel better is than gold:
In need thereof I stood.

Good counsel's good at any time;
The wise will it receive,
Tho' fools count he commits a crime
Who doth good counsel give.

I take it kindly at thy hand
Thou didst unto me write;
My feet upon Mount Zion stand,
In that take thou delight.

I am indeed in prison now
In body, but my mind
Is free to study Christ, and how
Unto me he is kind.

For tho' men keep my outward man
Within their locks and bars,
Yet by the faith of Christ I can
Mount higher than the stars.

Their fetters cannot spirits tame,
Nor tie up God from me;
My faith and hope they cannot lame;
Above them I shall be.

I here am very much refreshed
To think, when I was out
I preached life and peace and rest
To sinners round about.

My business then was souls to save
By preaching grace and faith,
Of which the comfort now I have,
And have it shall till death.

They were no fables that I taught,
Devis'd by cunning men,
But God's own word, by which were caught
Some sinners now and then.

Whose souls by it were made to see
The evil of their sin;
And need of Christ to make them free
From death, which they were in.

And now those very hearts that then
Were foes unto the Lord,
Embrace his Christ and truth, like men
Conquer'd by his word.

I hear them sigh, and groan, and cry
For grace to God above;
They loathe their sin, and to it die;
'Tis holiness they love.

This was the work I was about
When hands on me were laid;
'Twas this from which they pluck'd me out
And vilely to me said:

You heretic, deceiver, come,
To prison you must go;
You preach abroad, and keep not home,
You are the Church's foe.

But having peace within my soul,

And truth on every side,
I could with comfort them control,
And at their charge deride.

Wherefore to prison they me sent,
Where to this day I lie;
And can with very much content
For my profession die.

The prison very sweet to me
Hath been since I came here,
And so would also hanging be,
If God would there appear.

Here dwells good conscience, also peace;
Here be my garments white;
Here, though in bonds, I have release
From guilt, which else would bite.

When they do talk of banishment,
Of death, or such like things,
Then to me God send heart's content,
That like a fountain springs.

Alas! they little think what peace
They help me to, for by
Their rage my comforts do increase;
Bless God, therefore, do I.

If they do give me gall to drink,
Then God doth sweet'ning cast -
So much thereto that they can't think
How bravely it doth taste.

For as the devil sets before
Me heaviness and grief,
So God sets Christ and grace much more,
Whereby I take relief.

Though they say then that we are fools
Because we here do lie,
I answer, Jails are Christ his schools,
In them we learn to die.

'Tis not the baseness of this state
Doth hide us from God's face;
He frequently, both soon and late,
Doth visit us with grace.

Here come the angels, here come saints,
Here comes the Spirit of God,

To comfort us in our restraints
Under the wicked's rod.

God sometimes visits prisoners more
Than lordly palaces;
He often knocketh at the door
When he their houses miss.

The truth and life of heav'nly things
Lift up our hearts on high,
And carry us on eagles' wings
Beyond carnality.

It takes away those clogs that hold
The hearts of other men,
And makes us lively, strong and bold
Thus to oppose their sin.

By which means God doth frustrate
That which our foes expect -
Namely, our turning th' apostate,
Like those of Judas' sect.

Here comes to our remembrance
The troubles good men had
Of old, and for our furtherance
Their joys when they were sad.

To them that here for evil lie
The place is comfortless,
But not to me, because that I
Lie here for righteousness.

The truth and I were both here cast
Together, and we do
Lie arm in arm, and so hold fast
Each other; this is true.

This jail to us is as a hill,
From whence we plainly see
Beyond this world, and take our fill
Of things that lasting be.

From hence we see the emptiness
Of all the world contains;
And here we feel the blessedness
That for us yet remains.

Here we can see how all men play
Theirs parts, as on a stage -
How good men suffer for God's way,

And bad men at them rage.

Here we can see who holds that ground
Which they in Scripture find:
Here we see also who turns round
Like weathercocks with wind.

We can also from hence behold
How seeming friends appear
But hypocrites, as we are told
In Scripture everywhere.

When we did walk at liberty
We were deceiv'd by them,
Who we from hence do clearly see
Are vile, deceitful men.

These politicians that profess
For base and worldly ends,
Do not appear to us at best
But Machiavellian friends.

Though men do say we do disgrace
Ourselves by lying here
Among the rogues, yet Christ our face
From all such filth will clear.

We know there's neither flout nor frown
That we now for him bear,
But will add to our heavenly crown
When he comes in the air -

When he our righteousness forth brings
Bright shining as the day,
And wipeth off those sland'rous things
That scorners on us lay.

We sell our earthly happiness
For heavenly house and home;
We leave this world because 'tis less
And worse than that to come.

We change our drossy dust for gold,
From death to life we fly;
We let go shadows, and take hold
Of immortality.

We trade for that which lasting is,
And nothing for it give
But that which is already His
By whom we breathe and live.

That liberty we lose for him
Sickness might take away;
Our goods might also for our sin
By fire or thieves decay.

Again we see what glory 'tis
Freely to bear our cross
For Him who for us took up his
When he our servant was.

I am most free that men should see
A hole cut through my ear;
If others will ascertain me,
They'll hang a jewel there.

Just thus it is: we suffer here
For Him a little pain,
Who when he doth again appear
Will with him let us reign.

If all must either die for sin
A death that's natural,
Or else for Christ, 'tis best with him
Who for the last doth fall.

Who now dare say we throw away
Our goods or liberty,
When God's most holy word doth say
We gain thus much thereby?

Hark yet again, you carnal men,
And hear what I shall say
In your own dialect, and then
I'll you no longer stay.

You talk sometimes of valour much,
And count such bravely mann'd
That will not stick to have a touch
With any in the land.

If these be worth commending, then,
That vainly show their might,
How dare you blame those holy men
That in God's quarrel fight?

Though you dare crack a coward's crown,
Or quarrel for a pin,
You dare not on the wicked frown,
Nor speak against their sin.

For all your spirits are so stout
For matters that are vain,
Yet sin besets you round about;
You are in Satan's chain.

You dare not for the truth engage,
You quake at 'prisonment;
You dare not make the tree your stage
For Christ, that King potent.

Know, then, true valour there doth dwell
Where men engage for God
Against the Devil, death and hell,
And bear the wicked's rod.

These be the men that God doth count
Of high and noble mind;
These be the men that do surmount
What you in nature find.

First, they do conquer their own hearts,
All worldly fears, and then
Also the devil's fiery darts,
And persecuting men.

They conquer when they thus do fall,
They kill when they do die;
They overcome then most of all,
And get the victory.

The worldling understands not this,
'Tis clear out of his sight;
Therefore he counts this world his bliss,
And doth our glory slight.

The lubber knows not how to spring
The nimble footman's stage;
Neither can owls or jackdaws sing
When they are in the cage.

The swine doth not the pearls regard,
But them doth slight for grains,
Though the wise merchant labours hard
For them with greatest pains.

Consider, man, what I have said,
And judge of things aright;
When all men's cards are fully play'd,
Whose will abide the light?

Will those who have us hither cast?

Or they who do us scorn?
Or those who do our houses waste?
Or us who this have borne?

And let us count those things the best
That best will prove at last;
And count such men the only blest
That do such things hold fast.

And what tho' they us dear do cost,
Yet let us buy them so;
We shall not count our labour lost
When we see others' woe.

And let saints be no longer blam'd
By carnal policy,
But let the wicked be asham'd
Of their malignity.

John Bunyan – A Short Biography

John Bunyan was born appropriately enough at Bunyan's End in the parish of Elstow, near Bedford to Thomas and Margaret Bunyan. The exact date is unknown he was, however, baptized on November 30th, 1628.

By his own account, Bunyan in his youth enjoyed bell-ringing, dancing and playing games unfortunately sometimes on the Sunday Sabbath, these pleasures were to be later outlawed by the Puritan regime under Cromwell.

As a child Bunyan learned his father's trade of tinker (a mender of pots and pans) and was given some basic schooling. In his autobiographical work, Grace Abounding to the Chief of Sinners, Bunyan recorded little of his upbringing, but he did note how he picked up the habit of swearing from his father, suffered from nightmares, and read the popular stories of the day in cheap chap-books.

In the summer of 1644, shortly before his 16th birthday, Bunyan lost both his mother and his sister Margaret.

That autumn, Bunyan enlisted in the Parliamentary army after 225 recruits from the town of Bedford were demanded to fight in the Civil War. A muster roll for the garrison of Newport Pagnell shows him as private "John Bunnian". In Grace Abounding to the Chief of Sinners, he recounted an incident from this time, as evidence of the grace of God:

"When I was a Souldier I, with others were drawn out to go to such a place to besiege it; But when I was just ready to go, one of the company desired to go in my room, to which, when I had consented, he took my place; and coming to the siege, as he stood Sentinel, he was shot into the head with a Musket bullet and died."

Bunyan's army service provided him with a knowledge of military language which he used in his book The Holy War. These army years also exposed him to the ideas of the various religious sects and radical groups. The garrison town of Newport Pagnell also gave him opportunities to indulge in behaviour he would later confess to in Grace Abounding to the Chief of Sinners: "So that until I came to the state of Marriage, I was the very ringleader of all the Youth that kept me company, in all manner of vice and ungodliness".

Bunyan spent nearly three years in the army, leaving in 1647 to return to Elstow and a trade as a tinker.

Within two years of leaving service Bunyan married. The name of his wife and the date of his marriage are not recorded but Bunyan did write that his wife, a pious young woman, brought with her into the marriage two books that she had inherited from her father: Arthur Dent's Plain Man's Pathway to Heaven and Lewis Bayly's Practice of Piety. He claimed also that, apart from the books, the newly-weds possessed little: "not having so much household-stuff as a Dish or a Spoon betwixt us both".

The couple's first daughter, Mary, was born in 1650, and it soon became apparent that she was blind. They would have three more children, Elizabeth, Thomas and John.

It was only after his marriage that he developed a deeper interest in religion, attending, at first, the local parish church and then joining the Bedford Meeting, a non-conformist group in Bedford, where he became a preacher.

The story that has gained credence is that one Sunday the vicar of Elstow preached a sermon against Sabbath breaking, which Bunyan took to heart. One afternoon, as he was playing tip-cat (a game in which a small piece of wood is hit with a bat) on Elstow village green, he heard a voice from the heavens "Wilt thou leave thy sins, and go to Heaven? Or have thy sins, and go to Hell?" These next few years were filled with spiritual conflict as he struggled with doubts and fears over religion and the guilt of what he thought was his own state of sin.

His journey began when Bunyan happened to be in Bedford and passed a group of women talking about spiritual matters. They were founding members of the Bedford Free Church or Meeting and Bunyan, who had been attending the parish church of Elstow, was so impressed by their talk that he joined their church. At that time the non-conformist group was meeting in St John's church in Bedford under the leadership of former Royalist army officer John Gifford. At the instigation of other members of the congregation Bunyan began to preach, both in the church and to groups of people in the surrounding countryside.

In 1656, having by this time moved his family to St Cuthbert's Street in Bedford, he published his first book, Gospel Truths Opened, which was inspired by a dispute with Quakers.

Tragically in 1658 Bunyan's wife died, leaving him with four small children. The following year later he re-married to an eighteen-year-old woman called Elizabeth.

With the death of Cromwell, and with it the end of the Republic Charles II was restored to the throne in 1660. The religious tolerance which had allowed Bunyan the freedom to preach now became curtailed. The members of the Bedford Meeting were no longer able to meet in St John's church, which they had been sharing with the Anglican congregation.

That November, Bunyan was preaching at Lower Samsell, a farm near the village of Westoning, and was told there was a warrant was out for his arrest. Deciding not to effect an escape, he was arrested and brought before the local magistrate, Sir Francis Wingate, at Harlington House.

Under the reign of Charles II religious freedom was, ironically, no longer to be tolerated. Whilst the Act of Uniformity, which made it compulsory for preachers to be ordained by an Anglican bishop and the revised Book of Common Prayer to be used in church services, was still two years away, and the Act of Conventicles, which made it illegal to hold religious meetings of five or more people outside the Church of England was not passed until 1664.

The authorities had arrested Bunyan under the Conventicle Act of 1593, which made it an offence to attend a religious gathering other than at the parish church with more than five people outside their family. This offence was punishable by 3 months imprisonment followed by banishment or execution if the person then failed to promise not to re-offend. The Act had been little used, and Bunyan's arrest was probably due in part to concerns that non-conformist religious meetings were being held as a cover for people plotting against the king although there is no evidence to suggest that was the case with Bunyan's meetings.

His trial took place in January 1661 at the quarter sessions in Bedford, before a group of magistrates under John Kelynge (who would later help to draw up the Act of Uniformity). Bunyan, who had been held in prison since his arrest, was indicted of having "devilishly and perniciousy abstained from coming to church to hear divine service" and having held "several unlawful meetings and conventicles, to the great disturbance and distraction of the good subjects of this kingdom". He was sentenced to three months imprisonment with transportation to follow if at the end of this time he didn't agree to attend the parish church and desist from preaching.

Bunyan refused to agree to give up preaching and his period of imprisonment eventually extended to 12 years in Bedford County Gaol, which stood on the corner of the High Street and Silver Street. His stance caused great hardship to his family. Elizabeth, made many strenuous attempts to obtain his release, and had been pregnant when her husband was arrested and she subsequently gave birth prematurely to a still-born child. She was left to bring up four step-children and to rely on the charity of Bunyan's fellow members of the Bedford Meeting and supporters. Bunyan's only meagre earnings in gaol were from making shoelaces and contributed little to family finances.

Despite their precarious state Bunyan remained resolute: "O I saw in this condition I was a man who was pulling down his house upon the head of his Wife and Children; yet thought I, I must do it, I must do it".

However, on several occasions when he was allowed out of prison, depending on the gaolers or the mood of the authorities at the time, he was even to attend the Bedford Meetings and even preach. His daughter Sarah was born during his imprisonment (the other child of his second marriage, Joseph, was born after his release in 1672).

In prison, Bunyan had a copy of the Bible and of John Foxe's Book of Martyrs, and access to writing materials and the company of other preachers who had been imprisoned. During these dark years he wrote Grace Abounding to the Chief of Sinners and started work on The Pilgrim's Progress, as well as penning several tracts that may have brought him a little extra money. In 1671, while still in prison, he was chosen as pastor of the Bedford Meeting.

By now, with the monarchy allowing increasing religious toleration, the king issued, in March 1672, a declaration of indulgence which suspended penal laws against non-conformists. Thousands were released from prison, amongst them Bunyan shortly after in May. He immediately sought and obtained a licence to preach under the declaration of indulgence and devoted his time to writing and preaching. He continued as pastor of the Bedford Meeting and travelled on horseback to preach, becoming known affectionately as "Bishop Bunyan". His preaching also took him to London, where Lord Mayor Sir John Shorter became a friend and presented him with a silver-mounted walking stick.

The Pilgrim's Progress was published in 1678 by Nathaniel Ponder and was an immediate success and bringing the family some financial comfort. Indeed, Bunyan's later years, in spite of another short term of imprisonment, were spent in relative comfort as a popular author and preacher, and pastor of the Bedford Meeting.

In 1688, on his way to London, Bunyan detoured to Reading, Berkshire, to try and resolve a quarrel. After he continued to London to the house of his friend, the grocer John Strudwick of Snow Hill in the City of London. He was caught in a storm and fell ill with a fever.

John Bunyan died in Strudwick's house on the morning of 31st August, 1688. He was buried in Bunhill Fields non-conformist burial ground in London.

Bunyan's estate at his death was worth £42 19s 0d. His widow Elizabeth died 3 years later in 1691.

The Pilgrim's Progress is one of the most published books in the English language with almost 1,500 editions having been printed.

Between 1656 when he published his first work, Some Gospel Truths Opened, and his death in 1688, Bunyan published 42 titles. A further two works, including his Last Sermon, were published the following year by George Larkin.

In 1692 Southwark comb-maker Charles Doe, who was a friend of Bunyan's later years, brought out, a collection of the author's works, including 12 previously unpublished titles, mostly sermons. Eventually in total the Bunyan canon was 58 titles.

It is the allegory, The Pilgrim's Progress, that made Bunyan's name as an author and for which he is best remembered. During the 18th century Bunyan's rather raw style fell from favour, but his popularity returned with Romanticism, the poet Robert Southey writing an appreciative biography in 1830.

Bunyan's reputation was further enhanced by the evangelical revival and he became a favourite author of the Victorians. The tercentenary of Bunyan's birth, celebrated in 1928, ironically brought praise from his former adversary, the Church of England.

John Bunyan – A Selected Bibliography
Among Bunyan's many works:

A Few Sighs from Hell, or the Groans of a Damned Soul, 1658
A Discourse Upon the Pharisee and the Publican, 1685
A Holy Life
Christ a Complete Saviour (The Intercession of Christ And Who Are Privileged in It), 1692
Come and Welcome to Jesus Christ, 1678
Grace Abounding to the Chief of Sinners, 1666
Light for Them that Sit in Darkness
Praying with the Spirit and with Understanding too, 1663

Of Antichrist and His Ruin, 1692
Reprobation Asserted, 1674
Saved by Grace, 1675
Seasonal Counsel or Suffering Saints in the Furnace – Advice to Persecuted Christians in Their Trials & Tribulations, 1684
Solomon's Temple Spiritualized
Some Gospel Truths Opened, 1656
The Acceptable Sacrifice
The Desire of the Righteous Granted
The Doctrine of the Law and Grace Unfolded, 1659
The Doom and Downfall of the Fruitless Professor (Or The Barren Fig Tree), 1682
The End of the World, The Resurrection of the Dead and Eternal Judgment, 1665
The Fear of God – What it is, and what is it is not, 1679
The Greatness of the Soul and Unspeakableness of its Loss Thereof, 1683
The Heavenly Footman, 1698
The Holy City or the New Jerusalem, 1665
The Holy War – The Losing and Taking Again of the Town of Man-soul (The Holy War Made by Shaddai upon Diabolus, for the Regaining of the World), 1682
The Life and Death of Mr Badman, 1680
The Pilgrim's Progress, 1678
The Strait Gate, Great Difficulty of Going to Heaven, 1676
The Saint's Knowledge of Christ's Love, or The Unsearchable Riches of Christ, 1692
The Water of Life or The Richness and Glory of the Gospel, 1688
The Work of Jesus Christ as an Advocate, 1688